BRANCH LINES AROUND ASCOT

From Ash Vale, Weybridge, Staines and Wokingham

Vic Mitchell and Keith Smith

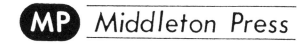

MP Middleton Press

*Cover picture details are
given in caption no. 108.*

Design – Deborah Goodridge

First published April 1989

ISBN 0 906520 64 9

© *Middleton Press, 1989*

Typeset by CitySet - Bosham 573270

*Published by Middleton Press
          Easebourne Lane
          Midhurst, West Sussex
          GU29 9AZ
          ☎ (0730) 813169*

*Printed & bound by Biddles Ltd,
          Guildford and Kings Lynn*

INDEX

CONTENTS

ACKNOWLEDGEMENTS

We are very grateful for the assistance received from many of the photographers mentioned in the captions and also for the help given by J. Barrett, R.M. Casserley, G. Croughton, N. Langridge, C.B. Mills, S.C. Nash, R. Randell, E. Staff, N. Stanyon, R. Turner, E. Wilmshurst and our ever helpful wives.

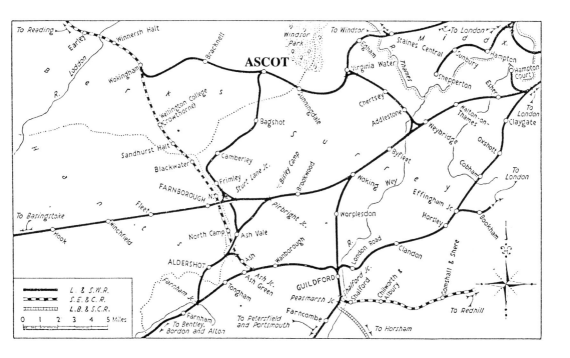

Map of the lines around Ascot, prior to 1923

(Railway Magazine)

GEOGRAPHICAL SETTING

Ascot is situated on the sands of the Bagshot Beds and the railways to it traverse these deposits together with the pebbles and sands of the Barton and Bracklesham Beds. This infertile sandy area between the valleys of the Blackwater River in the west and the River Thames in the east rises to over 400 ft. above sea level.

The line from Staines passes over the Flood-plain Gravels, in the Egham area, before reaching the high sands, while the route from Ash Vale initially runs parallel to the Blackwater River, on its associated alluvium, north to the Camberley area. Gradients of 1 in 60 are to be found for two miles either side of the summit, between Camberley and Bagshot. The 121 yd. long Bagshot Tunnel is ¼ mile north of the summit.

The route from Wokingham traverses mainly London Clay (ideal for brickmaking) before reaching Bracknell and the sands, while the Weybridge line runs along the eastern extremity of the sands, close to the Thames Valley.

Maps are to the scale of 25″ to 1 mile, unless otherwise stated.

HISTORICAL BACKGROUND

Most of the main line from London to Basingstoke was completed in 1838 and that to Windsor via Staines in 1848. These were to form the principal routes of the London & South Western Railway in the district. The South Eastern Railway line from London to Reading via Guildford and Wokingham came into use in stages during 1849.

The first of the lines covered by this album to be opened was that between Weybridge and Chertsey, traffic commencing on 14th February 1848.

The Staines to Wokingham line was authorised in 1853 and completed in 1856, being opened to Ascot on 4th June and west thereof on 9th July. The LSWR operated the route from the opening, leased it from the owning company from 1858 and acquired it in 1878.

The Chertsey branch was extended north to Virginia Water on 1st October 1866, triangular junctions eventually being provided at both ends of the route.

A single line was opened between Ascot and Ash Vale on 18th March 1878, it being doubled between Ascot and Frimley in 1893. Connections to the main Woking–Basingstoke line were provided in both directions and were double from the outset. The link line between Brookwood and Farnham had come into use on 2nd May 1870.

* * * * *

Electrification to Windsor took place in 1930 and on 3rd January 1937 it was extended from Staines to Weybridge, as part of the Portsmouth scheme. Electric services between Waterloo and Reading commenced on 1st January 1939 and from that date they were also operated from Ascot to Guildford via Camberley and Aldershot, where reversal was necessary.

WOKING and FARNHAM to ASCOT.—London and South Western.

Down.			Week Days.								Sundays			Up.				Week Days.								Sundays	
Waterloo,	mrn	mrn	mrn	mrn	aft	aft	aft	aft	aft	aft		mrn	aft		Waterloo,	mrn	mrn	mrn	mrn	aft	aft	aft	aft	aft	aft		mrn	aft
London 52 dep	6 55	...	...	9 0	1215	2 45	...	4 10	...	5 50		...	5 30		London 55 dep	7 35	...	9 38	...	1240	...	3 0	...	4 45	6 37		mrn	8 35
Woking ....dep	7 45	...	...	10 0	...	1 25	3 35	...	4 53	...	5	6 35		7 30	7 14	Ascot....dep	8 53	...	1115	...	2 35	...	4 30	...	5 52	8 20	...	9 50	10 0
Brookwood	7 53	...	...	10 7	...	1 32	3 42	...	5 0	...		6 42		7 37	7 21	Bagshot (Town *	9 1	...	1123	...	3 43	...	4 38	...	6 0	8 28	...	9 58	10 8
Farnham..dep	7 12	...	9 45	...	1 15	2 43	...	4 18	5 35	...	5 44				Camberly & York	9 9	9 15	1131	1137	2 51	2 56	...	4 46	5 0 6	9 8 35	8 39	10 6	1016
Aldershot	7 35	...	10 0	...	1 25	3 20	...	4 28	5 45	...	6 33		7 53	7 37	Frimley	9 13	9 19	1136	1141	2 56	3 0	...	4 51	5 5 6 13	3 39	8 44	1010	1021
North Camp ..	7 41	...	...	10 6	...	1 31	3 26	...	4 34	5 51	...	6 39		8 0	7 44	Frimley ...dep	9 20	...	1142	...	3 0	...	3 39	5 10	...	6 17	8 41	1010	1021
Frimley ...arr	7 45	...	...	1013	...	1 38	3 23	...	4 41	5 58	...	6 46		8 7	7 51	North Camp ..	9 27	...	1150	...	3 7	...	3 46	5 17	...	6 24	8 51	1017	1028
Frimley ....| 8 4	8 10	1014	1020	1 59	1 46	3 53	4 42	5 10	...	6 47	6 54		8 8	8 7	Aldershot ....| 9 33	...	1157	...	3 13	...	3 51	5 23	...	6 30	8 57	1022	1034
Camberly & York	8 10	8 15	1018	1025	1 43	1 52	3 53	4 46	5 15	...	6 51	6 59		8 13	7 57	Farnham 52 a	9 40	...	12 5	...	3 56	5 30	...	7 43	9 3	...	1037	...
Bagshot (Town *	8 21	...	...	1032	...	2 1 4	6	...	5 22	...	...	7 7		8 20	8 4	Brook'w'd 44.	9 23	...	1151	...	3 8	...	...	5 2	...	6 24	...	1040	1052
Ascot 55 ....arr	8 29	...	...	1040	...	2 9	4 13	...	5 29	...	...	7 15		8 26	8 10	Woking 52, 54 ar	9 29	...	1157	...	3 14	...	...	5 8	...	6 30	9 56	1046	1058
Waterloo 59 a	9 49	...	...	12 5	...	3 42	5 45	...	6 47	...	...	9 21		9 45	9 34	55 Waterloo arr	1024	...	1257	...	4 28	...	...	6 12	...	7 38	10 9	1152	...

* Station for Sandhurst.

PASSENGER SERVICES

Staines – Reading

	Staines – Reading		Staines – Ascot	
	Weekdays	Sundays	Weekdays	Sundays
1869	6	2	–	–
1890	10	3	1	–
1906	12	4	2	5
1917	13	3	4	1
1928	14	7	3	2

This table and the one below are intended to give an indication of the development of the timetable and do not include trains running on less than five days a week or on local journeys. In the final years of steam, a few of the services to Ascot were extended to Aldershot or Farnham.

Following the electrification of the Windsor line in 1930, steam services to Reading were rescheduled to hourly intervals, outside the business hours.

Weybridge – Virginia Water

	Weybridge – Virginia W.		Weybridge – Chertsey	
	Weekdays	Sundays	Weekdays	Sundays
1869	6	1	5	3
1890	13	6	6*	2
1906	16	6	10	4
1917	22	5	8	2
1928	20	7	9	4

*Includes a coach from Waterloo, slipped at Weybridge at 4.42 pm. This facility had been introduced in 1863 and lasted until 1903.

WINDSOR and WOKING.—London & South Western.											
	mrn	mrn	aft	aft	aft		mrn	mrn	aft	aft	aft
Windsor dep	6 30	9 50	1236	3 30	6 0	Woking..dep	8 35	1125	229	4 50	8 5
Datchet......	6 34	9 54	1241	3 34	6 4	Byfleet......	8 40	1130	225	4 55	8 10
Wraysbury..	6 39	9 59	1246	3 39	6 9	Addlestone..	8 48	1139	233	5 3	8 18
Staines (H St)	6 45	10 5	1250	3 45	615	Chertsey....	8 53	1143	239	5 8	8 23
Egham	6 50	1010	1255	3 50	620	Virginia Wtr	8 59	1149	247	5 14	8 30
Virginia Wtr	6 56	1016	1 0	3 56	626	Egham......	9 5	1155	253	5 20	8 36
Chertsey....	7 2	1022	1 5	4 2	632	Staines (H St)	9 10	12 0	258	5 25	8 41
Addlestone..	7 7	1027	1 9	4 7	637	Wraysbury..	9 16	12 6	3 4	5 31	8 47
Byfleet......	7 15	1035	1 17	4 14	645	Datchet......	9 21	1211	3 9	5 36	8 52
Woking..arr	7 20	1040	1 22	4 18	650	Windsor arr	9 25	1215	313	5 40	8 56

This 1890 timetable is typical of the Windsor – Woking service operated until World War I.

Camberley Line

In steam days, trains operated between Ascot and Woking or Farnham, as illustrated by the timetables. The service was of a branch line nature, with only two through trains to Waterloo being shown as late as 1938.

An unusual working in 1934 – 36 was a 12-noon departure from Ascot, calling at all stations to Winchfield. On some Saturdays it was extended to Basingstoke but there was no public return service.

Electric services

A 30 minute interval was provided, seven days a week. Camberley line passengers found a dramatic improvement in the London service from 2 to 36 trains daily. Apart from some war years, this interval has been maintained, at least on weekdays, although the points of division of the trains has varied in recent years.

From 1937 until 1976, Windsor trains shed a portion for Weybridge at Staines. Thereafter a shuttle service was operated and in 1986 alternate trains ran to Woking. Since May 1987 this service has been extended to Waterloo via Hounslow.

From 1939 until 1982, Reading trains divided at Ascot, where the rear portion departed for Guildford via Aldershot, where it reversed. 1982 – 88 saw a shuttle service between Ascot and Guildford since when alternate trains have operated through to Waterloo and to Reading, a sure way to attract passengers. Since May 1987, one of the two fast hourly trains to and from London has omitted the Staines stop.

The foregoing notes refer to the basic service which was often enhanced during the peak hours. For example, business travellers could reach Waterloo, via the main line through Surbiton, from Ascot and Camberley until September 1964 and continued to do so from Chertsey in 1989.

1. Ash Vale to Bagshot

ASH VALE

1. The station opened on 2nd May 1870, when the line between Brookwood and Farnham came into use. Until 30th March 1924, it was named "North Camp and Ash Vale". The parapet of the bridge over Frimley Road is visible, just beyond the down starting signal. (D. Cullum)

The 1915 map shows a boathouse on the Basingstoke Canal which passes under the line between the station and its junction. The water of Little Mytchett Flash is continuous with that of the canal, which is illustrated in pictures 39 to 43 of *Surrey Waterways*. (Middleton Press)

2. The up platform canopy had been extended east in a contrasting style whilst the down platform retained a boarded portion. Both photographs were taken in August 1966. (D. Cullum)

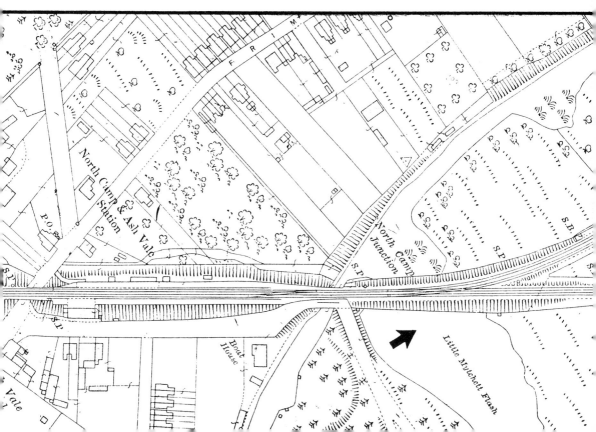

3. The 12.55 Alton to Waterloo service on 16th May 1969 was operated by green-painted unit no. 6138 and unit no. 6028, which contrasted in its blue livery. These are two of the 173 2HAP units built in 1957–58. The generous provision for gentlemen is evident in this picture. (J.H. Bird)

> **Other views of this station are to be seen in our *Woking to Alton* album in the Country Railway Routes series.**

4. Rebuilding of the station was finished in 1972, the booking office being situated in the subway, half way up from the road level. This is the view west in June 1988, when eight trains called each hour of basic service. (J. Scrace)

5. With the canal bridge in the foreground, 2HAL unit no. 2626 rumbles over the junction on 19th May 1969. It was working the 11.38 Waterloo to Guildford service, via Ascot, the direct route from Waterloo, via Woking, being on the right. (J.H. Bird)

6. Ash Vale Junction Box is by the 15 chain curve, north of the junction and remained in use in 1989, controlling colour light signals.

The driver of unit no. 2610 is seen preparing to surrender the tablet after leaving the single line section on 22nd March 1968. (J. Scrace)

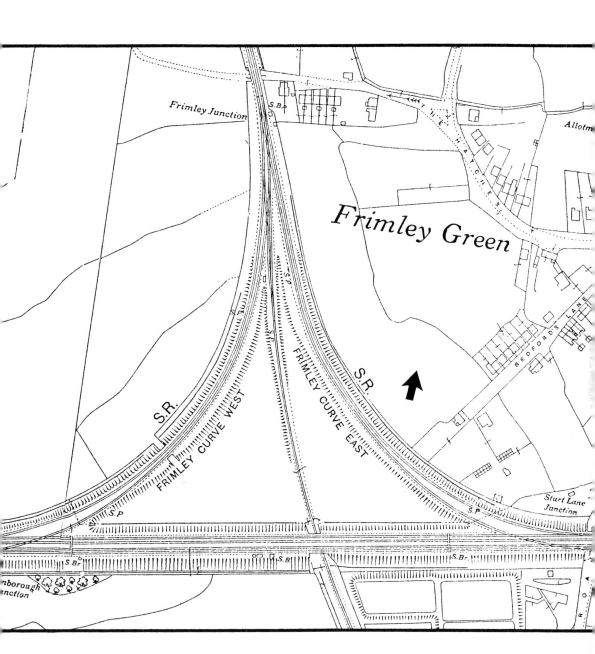

Frimley Junction

S.B.

THE HATCHES

Allotm

Frimley Green

S.R.

FRIMLEY CURVE WEST

S.R.

FRIMLEY CURVE EAST

BEDFORDS LANE

S.R.

S.P

S.P

S.P

Sturt Lane
Junction

S.Br

S.Br

S.Br

nborough
unction

R O A

7. Two miles north of Ash Vale, the single line passes under the quadruple tracks of the Waterloo–Basingstoke line. As is evident in this 1970 northward view, the bridge design and land purchase permit the provision of double track, if this should ever be required. (R.E. Ruffell)

The 1934 Survey shows the Woking to Basingstoke route from right to left and the single line from Ash Vale at the bottom. S.Br. indicates "Signal Bridge". These carried pneumatically operated signals, controlled from Sturt Lane Junction Box which is shown lower centre and is illustrated with picture no. 17 in our *Woking to Southampton* album. The scale is 20″ to 1 mile.

8. The signalman of Frimley Junction Box leans out to pass the single line token to the driver of the 1.54 pm Waterloo to Guildford service on 15th October 1955. The signal box remained in use until 25th March 1973. (D. Cullum)

→

10. The tablet is surrendered from London bound 4COR no. 3120 on 23rd October 1971. Both connections to the main line were taken out of use on 25th October 1964. The rails were soon lifted with the exception of one conductor rail which remained live to link the Frimley line with Sturt Lane sub-station. This dangerous object was eventually eliminated. (G.P. Cooper)

9. Looking south from the signal box on the same day, we see the main line and Sturt Lane Junction Box in the background, the connection to Brookwood on the left and that to Farnborough on the right. The commencement of the single line is in the centre of the picture. (D. Cullum)

FRIMLEY

11. A rather poor postcard view from the road bridge at least shows the relationship of the signal box to the goods yard. The station opened with the line but only a single platform was required until 1893. (Lens of Sutton)

12. Military movements were an important source of revenue for the railways of the area. Troops arrive in 1911, the train including flat wagons for guns, horse boxes and first class accommodation for officers, nearest the camera. (Lens of Sutton)

13. Although photographed over 50 years ago, this scene was little changed in 1989. The down platform retained its small canopy but the up building was boarded up due to vandalism. (Lens of Sutton)

14. Prior to electrification in 1939, a class M7 0-4-4T with a push-pull set was the common formation for passenger services. The clean insulators indicate that the transition was imminent. (Lens of Sutton)

15. On 18th October 1964, the RCTS and LCGB jointly operated a railtour to Midhurst to mark the total closure of the line from Petworth. It left Waterloo at 9.30 am and travelled via Ascot, Woking, Guild-

ford and Christs Hospital, returning via Littlehampton and Brighton, all for 37s 6d (£1.87½). Class S15 no. 30839 was used from London and three other locomotives worked different parts of the tour. (T. Wright)

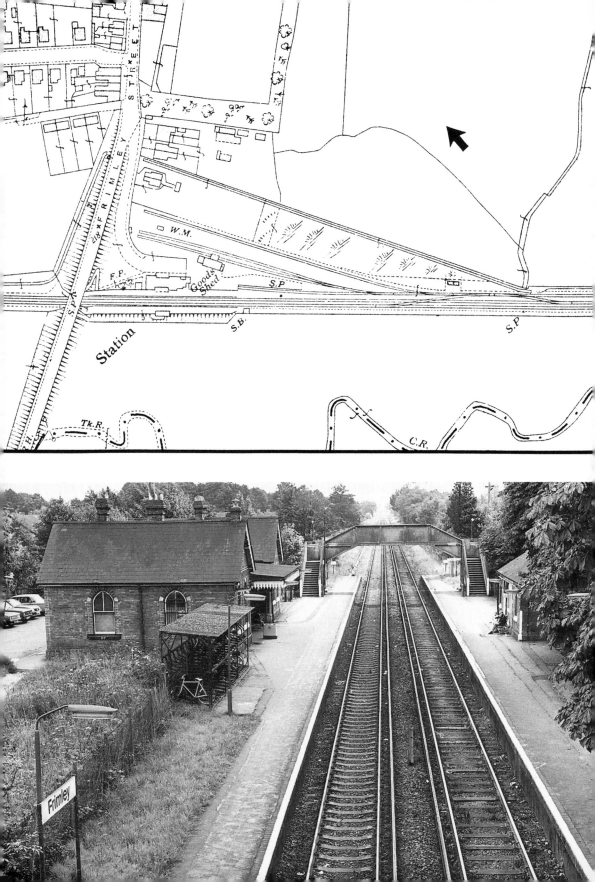

The 1934 edition includes the four sidings of the goods yard, which closed on 2nd April 1962. The goods shed contained a 30 cwt. capacity crane. West of the station (off the map) was the terminus of the 10¼″ gauge Surrey Border & Camberley Railway which operated in 1938–39. Through bookings from many SR stations were available. The railway is illustrated in our *Reading to Guildford* album – see photographs nos. 61 to 67.

16. In 1988, the station retained much of its rural ambience despite the nearby busy modern shopping street. Four coach trains normally operate, so short platforms still sufficed. (J. Scrace)

17. The gable ends bear stones carved *LSW 1877* and shortly after this photograph was taken in August 1988, renovation work commenced to enhance this link with a bygone age. (J. Scrace)

CAMBERLEY

18. An interesting picture from the signal box, before the erection of the footbridge and new down side buildings, includes the postman emptying the up-platform box. The suffix "& York Town" was in use until 1923. The platform canopies were extended in 1898 and a footbridge was added in 1902. (Lens of Sutton)

19. A very wide canopy was provided when new buildings were erected on the down platform. Apart from a fine display of moustaches, other items of interest are the gates devoid of warning targets, the brick abutment awaiting a footbridge and non-standard ballasting. (Lens of Sutton)

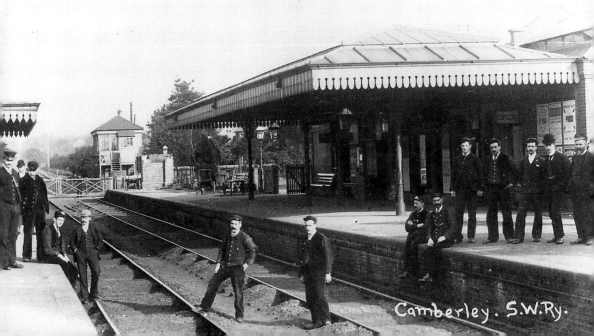

Camberley. S.W.Ry.

20. The chimneys on the up side are worthy of study and comparison with later photographs. Booking offices were provided on both sides of the station for some years. (Lens of Sutton)

The 1934 map emphasises the difficulty of working the yard with sidings much longer than the headshunt. C marks the position of the 5 ton capacity crane. The yard closed on 3rd May 1965.

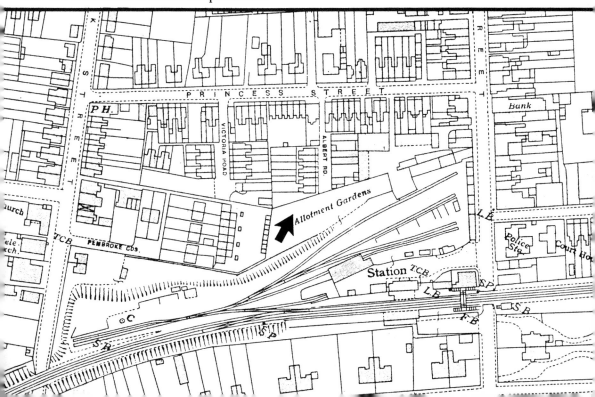

21. Class T1 no. 65 came to grief in January 1907 while shunting in the goods yard, the shunting neck being only 140 ft. long. Unfortunately, the locomotive records do not give any details of its excursion into Park Street. (Lens of Sutton)

23. The point giving access to the goods yard is visible behind 2HAL no. 2650 as it arrives with the 15.04 Guildford to Waterloo service on 19th May 1969. HAL indicated that **HA**lf of the train had a **L**avatory, i.e. only one coach was so provided. (J.H. Bird)

22. The stovepipe chimney of one of Mr. Adam's locomotives is evident as it prepares to depart for Ascot. The High Street has been redeveloped beyond recognition. (Lens of Sutton)

24. The up side exterior was similar to the main buildings at the adjacent stations, both of which survived in 1989. On the extreme left is the sub-station that was erected adjacent to the signal box. The photograph was taken on 12th September 1973, four years before the structure was demolished. (J. Scrace)

ASCOT to FARNHAM and WOKING.—London and South Western.

Miles.	Waterloo Station,	mrn	mrn	mrn	mrn	mrn	aft	mrn	aft	aft	aft	aft (Except Saturdays)	aft (Saturdays only)	aft	aft	aft	aft	aft	aft	aft	aft	aft	aft	SUNDAYS. mrn	mrn	aft
	151 London ....dep.	....	7 0	....	8 0	10 0	....	11 5	....	....	1 10	....	1 40	3g10	....	4 40	4 45	....	....	6 25	6 40	8 10	....	8 35	9 45	9 30
	Ascot ....dep.	....	8 22	8 38	10 27	11 20	....	12 33	....	....	2 35	....	3 7	4 45	....	5 29	5 55	....	....	7 17	8 40	9 40	....	9c50	11 16	10 36
3¼	Bagshot	....	8 29	8 45	10 34	11 27	....	12 41	1 38	....	2 42	2 54	3 14	4 52	5 7	5 36	6 2	....	7 0	7 24	8 48	9 47	....	9 57	11 23	10 44
6¼	Camberley & York Town*	7 35	8 39	8 53	10 41	11 36	....	12 50	1 46	....	2 51	3 2	3 22	5 1	5 15	5 46	6 11	....	7 8	7 33	8 57	9 55	12 0	10 5	11 31	10 52
8¾	Frimley	7 41	8 45	8 59	10 50	11 42	....	12 57	1 52	....	2 57	3 8	3 28	5 7	5 21	5 52	6 17	....	7 14	7 39	9 4	10 1	....	10 11	11 37	10 58
11¾	North Camp ¶ .....arr.	....	....	9 6	....	11 49		....	1 59	....	....	3 15	3 35	....	5 28	5 59	....	....	7 21	arr. at 8 14 aft. Basingstoke	....	10 8	....	10 18	11 44	11 5
14¼	Aldershot	....	....	9 12	....	11 56		....	2 5	....	....	3 20	3 41	....	5 33	6 5	....	....	7 27		....	10 13	12 16	10 24	11 50	11 11
17¼	130 **Farnham** .....arr.	....	....	9 19	....	12 3		....	....	....	....	3 28	3 49	....	....	6 12	....	....	7 34		....	10 22	12 22	....	11 57	....
—	North Camp ¶ .....dep.	....	....	9 26	....	11 57	12 10	....	2 12	2 41	....	4 15	4 15	....	6 11	6 11	....	6 24	7 33		....	10 37	....	10 31	12 8	11 19
13¾	Brookwood .... [130	7 50	8 53	9 35	10 59	12 5	....	1 5	2 21	2 50	3 6	4 23	4 23	5 16	....	....	6 26	6 34	7 42		9 13	10 45	....	10 39	12 16	11 27
17¼	**Woking** 102, 108, 122, arr	7 57	9 0	9 42	11 6	12 14	....	1 12	....	2 56	3 13	4 31	4 31	5 23	....	....	6 33	6 41	7 50		9 20	10 52	....	10 46	12 23	11 34
42	122 Waterloo ......arr.	8 44	9 47	10 19	11 55	1 35	12 58	2 26	3 6	3 47	4 15	5 30	5 30	6 50	7 0	7 0	7 50	7 50	8 46		10 30	11 40	....	12 4	1 47	....

Miles.	Waterloo Station,	mrn	mrn	mrn	mrn	mrn	mrn	mrn	aft	aft	aft	aft	aft	aft	aft	aft	aft	ngt. (Thursday morning)					SUNDAYS. mrn	mrn	aft
	120 London ....dep	5 50	6 0	7 20	8 0	9 20	10 5	11 45	12 8	1 10	2 28	3 5	4 12	5 5	6 0	7 15	10 30	12 25a	....	....	....	....	....	11 15	6 0
	Woking ....dep.	6 40	6 44	7 57	9 18	10 8	11 10	12 30	1 24	1 58	3 32	3 55	5 0	5 58	6 47	8 17	11 15	1 12	....	....	....	....	7c15	12 0	6c41
3¾	Brookwood	6 48	6 53	8 6	9 26	....	11 18	12 39	1 32	2 7	3 40	4 5	5 8	6 6	6 54	8 25	11 23	....	....	....	....	....	7 23	12 8	6 52
8¼	North Camp ¶ .....arr.	....	7 3	8 16	....	10 22	....	12 50	....	2 18	....	4 16	....	6 16	....	8 34	11 32	....	....	....	....	....	7 32	12 18	7 4
—	**Farnham** ....dep.	....	7 42	8 30	....	10 14	....	12 50	....	1 54	....	4 25	....	6 9	....	8 40	11 25	....	....	....	....	....	....	12 30	....
—	Aldershot	....	7 52	8 38	....	10 25	....	12 58	....	2 19	....	4 34	....	6 23	....	8 50	11 34	....	....	....	....	....	7 44	12 40	7 15
—	North Camp ¶ .....dep	....	7 57	8 44	....	10 30	....	1 4	....	2 25	....	4 40	....	6 29	....	8 56	11 40	....	....	....	....	....	7 50	12 48	7 22
8¾	Frimley	6 58	8 4	....	9 39	10 37	11 28	1 11	1 42	2 32	3 50	4 47	5 18	6 37	7 5	9 3	11 47	1 27	....	....	....	....	7 57	12 56	7 31
11	Camberley & York Town*	7 7	8 10	8 56	9 46	10 43	11 34	1 17	1 47	2 37	3 56	4 53	5 23	6 42	7 11	9 9	11 52	1 32	....	....	....	....	8 3	1 1	7 38
14¼	Bagshot	7 15	8 18	9 5	9 53	10 50	11 42	1 24	1 55	2s45	4 4	5 0	5 32	6 49	7 19	9 17	....	....	....	....	....	....	8 11	1 9	7 50
17½	**Ascot** 151 ....arr.	7 20	8 25	9 11	9 59	10 56	11 48	....	2 1	2s53	4 11	....	5 38	....	7 25	9 23	....	....	....	....	....	....	8 17	1 16	7 58
46½	151 Waterloo ......arr.	8 53	9 38	10 0	11 11	12 11	1 40	....	3 33	4s48	5b50	....	7 0	....	9 30	11 49	....	....	....	....	....	....	9 51	3 2	9 14

NOTES.

a Wednesday midnight.

b Arrives at 5 34 aft. on Saturdays.

c Via Aldershot.

g Leaves at 3 15 aft. on Saturdays.

s Saturdays only.

* Station for Sandhurst (1½ miles).

¶ North Camp and Ash Vale.

1906

25. The gates were replaced by full lifting barriers on 25th March 1973 and from February 1975 they were controlled from Feltham under CCTV. The signal box be- came a ground frame on 8th September 1974 and was closed totally in the following January. (J. Scrace)

26. Another 1988 photograph shows that the site of the former sidings was by then largely occupied by offices. 4VEP no. 3071 shows that the up platform is only suitable for four coaches. (J. Scrace)

BAGSHOT

27. Seen in LSWR livery, the station is little changed today. The chimneys have been modified and the *GENTLEMENS* demolished. (Lens of Sutton)

28. WD 2-10-0 no. 600 *Gordon* passes the 30 cwt. crane on 16th April 1966 as it returns the RCTS special train from Bentley. (See picture no. 106 in *Woking to Alton* for further details). A glimpse is obtained of the goods yard, which was closed on 3rd January 1966. (J.H. Bird)

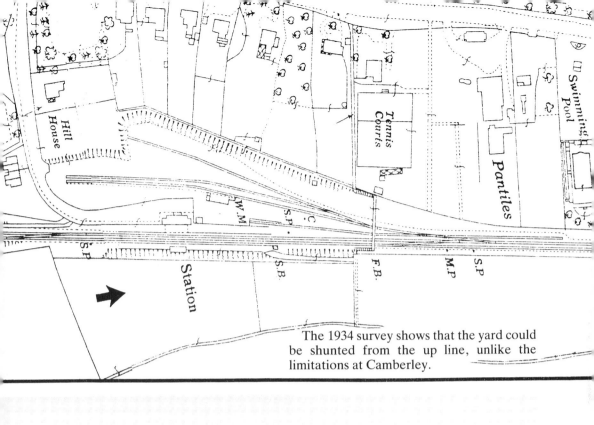

The 1934 survey shows that the yard could be shunted from the up line, unlike the limitations at Camberley.

29. 2HAL no. 2603 forms the 13.28 Waterloo
to Guildford service on 6th May 1970 and is
devoid of a number stencil, the painted headcode number being incorrect. The remaining
siding and crossover were lifted the following
year. (J. Scrace)

30. Viewed from the goods yard in 1970,
the pleasant rural station displays its poly-
chromatic brickwork. In 1989, the nearest
part remained in use as a booking office,
the remainder being let for commercial
purposes. (J. Scrace)

31. Another 1970 view includes the signalman going off duty, his box being abolished
on 3rd July 1973. Apart from this loss, the
scene was little altered nearly 20 years on.
(R.E. Ruffell)

2. Weybridge to Chertsey

WEYBRIDGE

32. The first station was opened over 150 years ago, on 21st May 1838. Looking towards London, prior to 1885, we see the later improvements which included a bay platform for the Chertsey branch, on the right. In 1885, an additional down line was laid, the resulting island platform being lost during the quadrupling, which was completed in 1902. Unlike most overbridges, this one did not require widening. (Lens of Sutton)

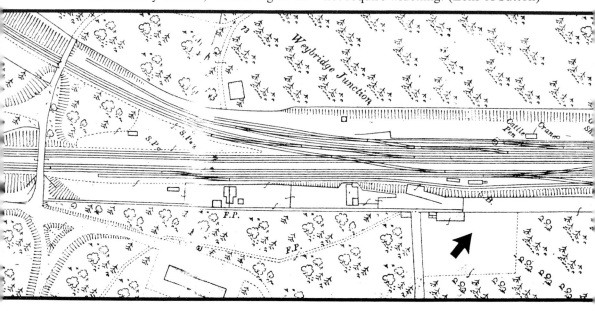

33. The sign refers to St. Georges Hill, an area housing many first class season ticket holders and including woodland of the type seen in the background. Class T9 no. 284 heads eight coaches and a van on the up slow line on 30th April 1927. (H.C. Casserley)

The 1914 map is worthy of study in conjunction with the 1870 and 1896 editions reproduced in our *Waterloo to Woking* album, adjacent to pictures 101–105. The bridge on the left carried a private road from *Brooklands*, a large country house north of the line, to the motor race track and airfield of the same name.

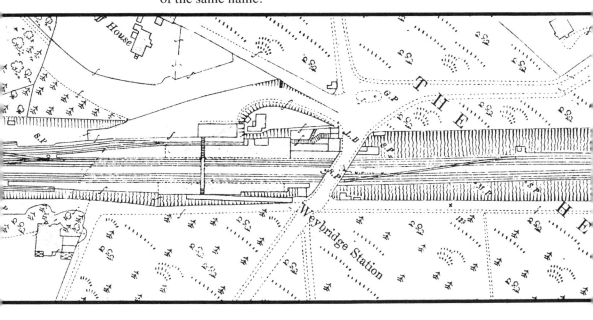

34. A picture from July 1950 makes an interesting comparison with the one before last and shows the 1902 booking office and footbridge. Since electrification, Chertsey line trains have departed from the up bay, the exception being a few through services from Waterloo in the peak hours. The unit is no. 1868, a 2NOL – two cars with NO Lavatories. (D. Cullum collection)

35. The shuttle service to Staines on 16th December 1977 was operated by no. 74005 with a 4TC set, owing to interruption of third rail current supplies. This was one of a small batch of electric locomotives built for the Kent Coast electrification scheme but by then converted to diesel operation. (R.E. Ruffell)

36. A push-pull unit leaves Weybridge Junction for the Chertsey branch, the nearby allotments sprouting one lattice and two wooden signal posts. The line on the left is the goods yard headshunt. (Lens of Sutton)

37. At the same location as the previous picture, unit no. 5682 uses the branch cross-over at the end of the reversible line from the bay platform, on 15th May 1969. The goods yard once had a crane of 4½ ton capacity and was closed on 3rd August 1964. (J. Scrace)

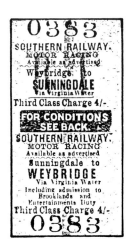

Less than ½ mile north of the Addlestone Junction, the line crosses the River Wey Navigation, close to Coxes Lock. The 1934 map shows the mill's private siding, which commenced near Addlestone level crossing and was opened in about 1904. Water transport of grain was out of favour for many years but, in September 1980, the 34 ton *Anny* began moving 60 ton loads from Tilbury Docks, twice a week. For about three centuries, the mill produced cannon balls and barrel hoops for the navy and only in its final 100 years or so did it produce flour. After several years of disuse, the siding closed on 27th May 1980 and the building was converted for residential use in 1989.

38. Addlestone Junction Box was at the northern apex of the triangular junction with the main line. This northward view was recorded in 1969, the box closing on 22nd March 1970. (J. Scrace)

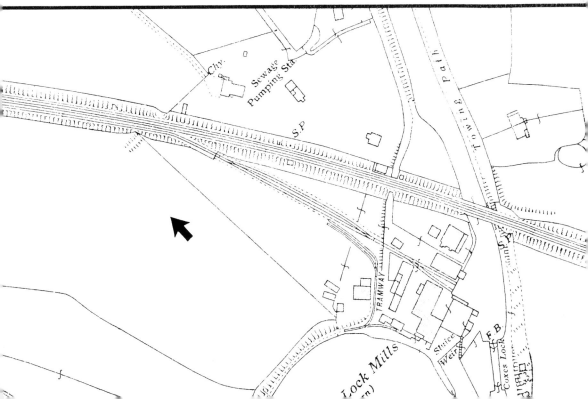

ADDLESTONE

39. An indifferent postcard shows a train arriving from Chertsey, with canopy reconstruction in progress to the left of it. Until 31st January 1937, the line in each direction from Chertsey was designated UP but from that date (i.e. electrification), UP referred to the entire route **from** Weybridge (or Byfleet Junction) **to** Virginia Water. (Lens of Sutton)

The 1934 map shows the extent of the goods yard, which closed on 15th December 1966, and the position of the 7½ ton crane.

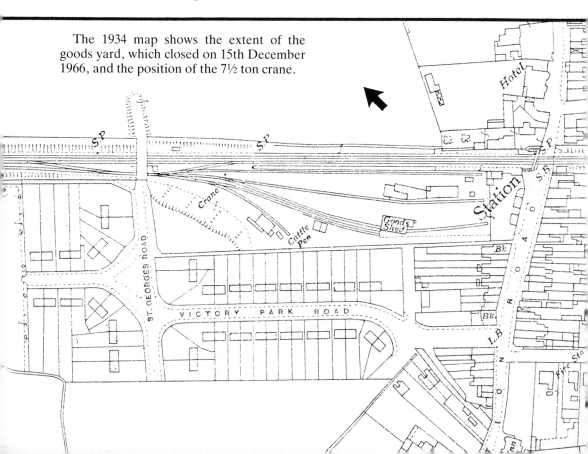

40. Another pre-electrification view, but looking south, shows the extent of the massive canopies. Residential development was stimulated by the railway and, by 1970, the population was in excess of 15,000. (Lens of Sutton)

41. The signal box was closed on 23rd January 1975, having been reduced to a gate box in September 1974. Class L11 no. 435, in SR livery, runs north with the sixth van of its train passing over the points of Coxes Lock Mill siding. The headcode indicates Southampton Docks to Nine Elms via Woking, Chertsey and Brentford. (D. Cullum collection)

42. Two 1988 views reveal the transition to minimum maintenance structures. Full lifting barriers replaced the gates on 13th May 1973 and, since 6th January 1974, they have been controlled from Surbiton Panel Box, under CCTV. (J. Scrace)

43. Introduced in 1985, class 455 units have operated most services in recent years, alternate trains terminating at Weybridge and Woking. Unfortunately for the business traveller, the Woking link has not operated in the peak hours. (J. Scrace)

CHERTSEY

44. Chertsey was the terminus of the branch from Weybridge from 1848 until 1866, the first station being east of the level crossing, on the site of the later goods yard. (Lens of Sutton)

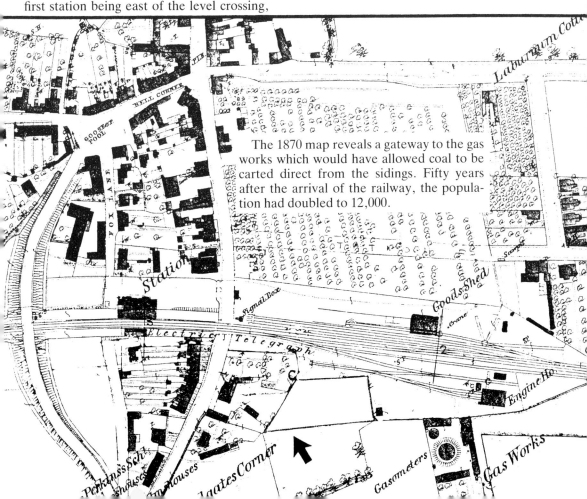

The 1870 map reveals a gateway to the gas works which would have allowed coal to be carted direct from the sidings. Fifty years after the arrival of the railway, the population had doubled to 12,000.

45. During the steam era for passenger trains, many Weybridge services terminated at Chertsey but here we see a through push-pull working from Virginia Water to Weybridge on 1st March 1931. The locomotive is seen better in the next photograph, taken earlier the same day. (H.C. Casserley)

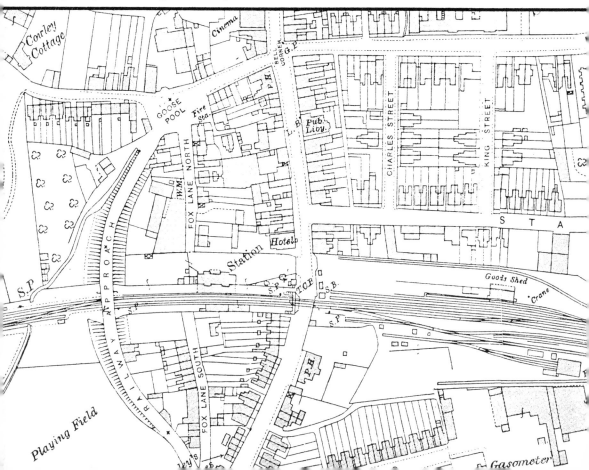

46. The two-road depot was a sub-shed of Strawberry Hill until Feltham was established in 1921. It had its own well and pump to supply the water tank and closed with the advent of electric services on 3rd January 1937. The locomotive coal is in wagons owned by Stevenson, Clarke & Co. Ltd. (H.C. Casserley)

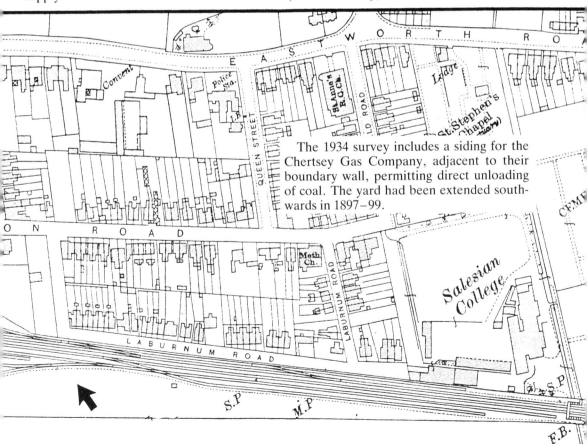

The 1934 survey includes a siding for the Chertsey Gas Company, adjacent to their boundary wall, permitting direct unloading of coal. The yard had been extended southwards in 1897–99.

47. Heavy freight trains to and from Feltham Marshalling Yard were once an important feature of the line. Class 700 no. 352 proceeds to Woking and passes the points leading to the electrified carriage sidings.
(Lens of Sutton)

48. On 15th June 1947, the 6.21 am freight train from Basingstoke to Feltham, hauled by class S15 4-6-0 no. 508, ran into the rear of 4SUB unit no. 4146, waiting in the up platform to start its journey to Waterloo at 7.42 am. Being a Sunday morning, there were no passengers and only the fireman suffered minor injury. The driver was held largely to blame. (British Rail)

S. E. & C. R.
TICKET FOR ONE BICYCLE PERAMBULATOR
OR CHILDREN'S MAIL CART.
Accompanied & at OWNER'S RISK
WOKINGHAM to

1640   1640

_____ Station.

Rate 9d.   See Back

49. The goods yard closed on 5th October 1964 but the goods shed was still complete when photographed in June 1966. The electrified siding diverges into two in the distance. These remained in use until May 1974, when new sidings became available at Staines. The gates were replaced by lifting barriers on 29th October 1972 and the signal box closed on 22nd January 1975, having been reduced to a gate box four months earlier. (D. Cullum)

50. A northward view from the footbridge in August 1988 reveals that at least the down side buildings retained their earlier dignity. Beyond the bridge, a loop was provided on the up side from 1896 until 1967. It was equipped with a conductor rail. (J. Scrace)

51. The handsome exterior was in good order in 1988 and makes an interesting comparison with the up side building at Staines, which is of similar plan but with plainer window frame surrounds. (J. Scrace)

52. The gas-lit Lyne Crossing was one mile north west of Chertsey and was fitted with automatic half barriers on 21st August 1966, when the signal box was closed. Here we look towards Virginia Water in March 1966. The crossing was abolished in 1976 when local roads were rearranged in connection with the construction of the M25. The railway was diverted from December 1976 until February 1979 to allow the building of an unusual skewed cable-stayed bridge, which would carry it over the new motorway. (D. Cullum)

3. Staines to Sunningdale

STAINES

53. A train from Reading crosses the junction with the Windsor line on 16th January 1927. The locomotive is 1893-built class A12 no. E625, E referring to Eastleigh. The SR had three sets of numbers at this time, the others being prefixed A or B on engines of Ashford or Brighton origin. (H.C. Casserley)

The 1866 survey, at 20″ to 1 mile, reveals the rural location of the station and the full extent of the small goods yard. Lower right are the buildings of Gresham Farm. The 1848 Windsor line is top left and the 1856 line to Ascot is below it.

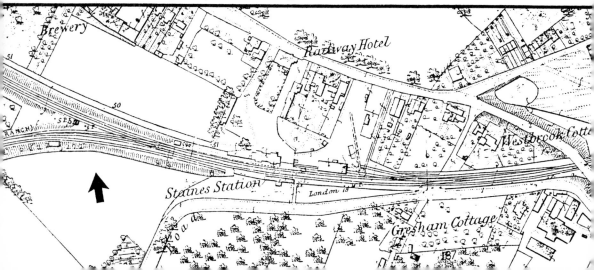

54. On 9th August 1957, unit no. 5225, forming the 12.02pm Weybridge to Waterloo service, started away with the up platform starting signal at danger and collided with class 700 no. 30688, which was crossing from the East yard to the down line. The four tracks of the yard are largely obscured by smoke. On the right is the 1930 signal box, which was closed on 8th September 1974. (British Rail)

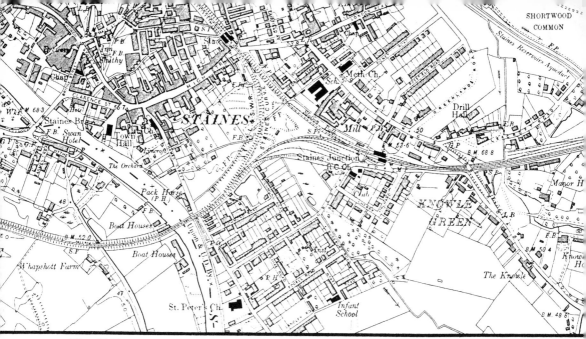

The 1920 map at 6″ to 1 mile shows the location of East Yard and West Yard, either side of Staines Junction station. This name was in use from 1885 until 1923, the suffix "Central" then being applied until January 1966. Also shown is the High Street station, on the Windsor line, which was open from 1884 until 1916. West Box was in the triangle of the junction while East Box was near to its 1930 successor, opposite East Yard. The GWR station is included, top left, this being the terminus of the branch from West Drayton.

55. A view from the same footbridge but about 40 years later, includes wagons in the West Yard, two 2BILs departing for Ascot and empty electric stock standing in one of the two carriage sidings. These sidings were in use until 1975. (T. Wright)

56. In 1974, the East Yard was relaid and electrified for EMU berthing. This 1979 view includes the two-coach Weybridge shuttle which waited in a siding between trips. The freight facilities at both yards were withdrawn on 31st August 1971. (R.E. Ruffell)

57. The junction signal is visible at the end of the down platform. The routes to Chertsey, Frimley and Bracknell have been controlled from Feltham Panel since 1974. Unit 5751 is working the 10.30 from Weybridge on 3rd September 1980. (R.E. Ruffell)

58. No. 47288 hauls empty petrol tank cars, bound for Ripple Lane, on 13th October 1984. The train had originated at Earley, between Wokingham and Reading, where the siding was closed on 25th July 1988.

Shopping development has taken place on the site of the third side of the triangular junction (*STAINES CURVE* on the map) which was in use from 7th April 1877 until 18th March 1965. (A. Dasi-Sutton)

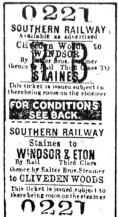

60. Egham Causeway crossing was little used on 11th December 1967, judging by the lack of wheel marks in the snow. It was closed completely on 29th September 1970. The gates were normally kept closed to road traffic, the exception being election days, when it was specially manned. (D. Cullum)

59. Thorpe Lane crossing, over the B388, is ¾ mile from Staines and is seen from the up side on 11th December 1967. Barriers came into use on 29th January 1973 and the box ceased to be a block post in September 1974. From 3rd March 1975, the barriers were operated under CCTV from Feltham. (D. Cullum)

61. Pooley Green crossing is ½ mile east of Egham and was fitted with automatic half barriers on 8th May 1977. The signal box was closed at the same time. Unit no. 7387 is bound for Guildford on 12th September 1973 and is about to pass the site of the future M25 overbridge. (J. Scrace)

EGHAM

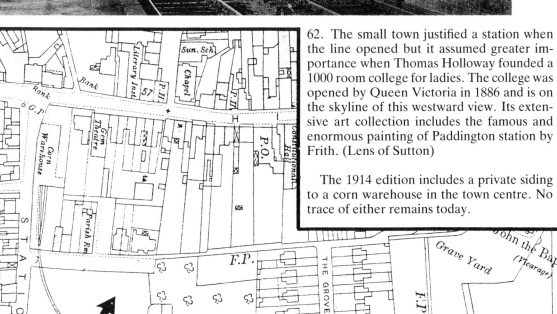

62. The small town justified a station when the line opened but it assumed greater importance when Thomas Holloway founded a 1000 room college for ladies. The college was opened by Queen Victoria in 1886 and is on the skyline of this westward view. Its extensive art collection includes the famous and enormous painting of Paddington station by Frith. (Lens of Sutton)

The 1914 edition includes a private siding to a corn warehouse in the town centre. No trace of either remains today.

63. The spacious goods shed is evident in this view towards London. The up platform canopy, on the left, was later replaced with a single pitched one. (Lens of Sutton)

64. Two 2NOLs form an up train on 1st April 1940, as a typical through freight service proceeds west. The signal box controlled gates until 3rd December 1972 when full lifting barriers were installed. It was reduced to a gate box on 8th September 1974 and was abolished on 10th February 1975, since when the crossing has been supervised by CCTV from Feltham panel.
(D.H. Wakely/J.R.W. Kirkby)

65. An eastward view from the same footbridge on the same day shows class H16 no. 516 thundering up the 1 in 1641 gradient from the Thames Valley, with a Feltham to Reading freight transfer. The crane had a 10 ton capacity, an improvement on the small one in photograph no. 62.
(D.H. Wakely/J.R.W. Kirkby)

66. On 28th November 1965, Portsmouth main line services were diverted via Chertsey. The goods yard, which closed on 4th January 1965, had once handled the heavy engineering products of Foster Wheeler.
(R.E. Ruffell)

67. By 1974, the exterior of the station had become rather drab and plans were being made for new buildings. The road approach would sadly not be as spacious as we see here.
(J. Scrace)

68. The new station was officially opened by Lady Lawrence on 24th July 1985 and was still clean and well kept when photographed in June 1988. The waiting room contained a commendable selection of railway photographs. (J. Scrace)

69. ¾ mile west of Egham is Rusham Crossing, which was being fitted with automatic half barriers when photographed on 16th July 1966. The box could be converted to a block post when the timetable so required. The next crossing west was Stroud, which had been downrated to a footpath in 1950. (J.J. Smith)

70. The station was opened with the line for the benefit of visitors to the lake and the scattered local community. Virginia Water is over 1½ miles long and a similar distance from the station. It was created in about 1750 by damming The Bourne which flows to the Thames, through Chertsey. The up platform canopy can be seen between the station and the Railway Hotel. (Lens of Sutton)

72. Looking towards Staines, the tops of two wagons are visible on the left. The two siding goods yard closed on 2nd May 1960. Passenger traffic was boosted by another of Thomas Holloway's philanthropic exercises. North of the station, he was involved in the building of an extensive mental hospital, St. Ann's Heath Sanatorium. (Lens of Sutton)

71. The small waiting shelter probably predates the Chertsey line, on the left. 'A' Box is in the centre of the picture and 'B' Box is in the distance. Virginia Water is at the southern border of Windsor Great Park and close to the equally famous Wentworth Golf Course. (Lens of Sutton)

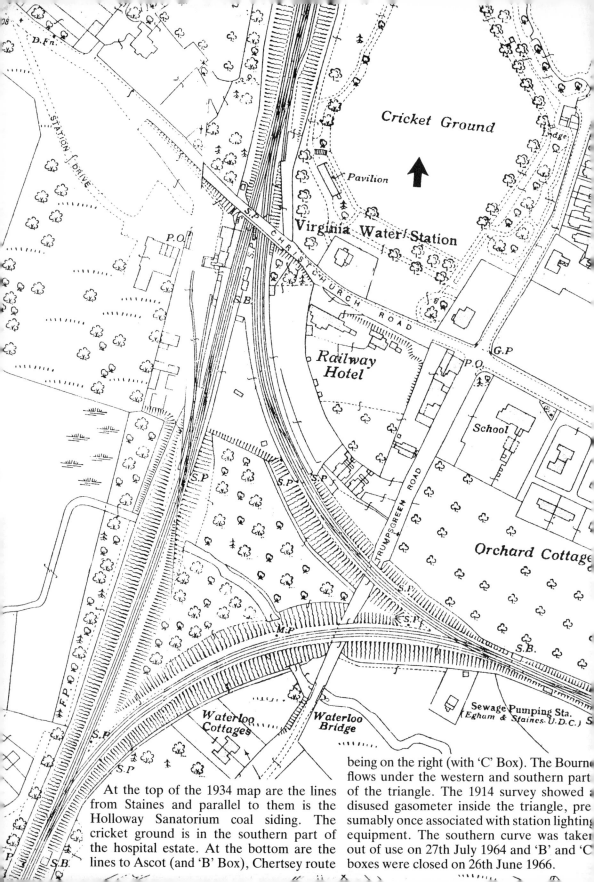

Cricket Ground

Pavilion

Virginia Water Station

Railway Hotel

School

Orchard Cottage

Waterloo Cottages

Waterloo Bridge

Sewage Pumping Sta.
(Egham & Staines U.D.C.)

STATION DRIVE

CHRISTCHURCH ROAD

TRUMPSGREEN ROAD

D.Fn.

P.O.

S.B.

S.P

S.P

S.P

S.P

S.P

M.P

S.P

S.B.

F.P

Lodge

G.P

P.O.

At the top of the 1934 map are the lines from Staines and parallel to them is the Holloway Sanatorium coal siding. The cricket ground is in the southern part of the hospital estate. At the bottom are the lines to Ascot (and 'B' Box), Chertsey route being on the right (with 'C' Box). The Bourne flows under the western and southern part of the triangle. The 1914 survey showed a disused gasometer inside the triangle, presumably once associated with station lighting equipment. The southern curve was taken out of use on 27th July 1964 and 'B' and 'C' boxes were closed on 26th June 1966.

73. A 1934 photograph features class 700 no. 315 taking the Chertsey line and forcing its way round the 10 chain curve. This severe curve presents gap problems at the platform edge for passengers and still necessitates a 15 mph speed restriction. (C.R.L. Coles)

74. There were few visitors during WWII, as Virginia Water was drained out to confuse enemy aviators. In 1947, the 500 acre Valley Gardens was started, containing a wide variety of flowering shrubs and ornamental trees. Maybe some additional railway passengers resulted – they were certainly numerous when photographed in 1953. (D. Cullum)

75. The 10.12 am Waterloo to Weybridge has just finished its one mile climb at 1 in 150 on 16th June 1953, having shed the Windsor portion at Staines. On the right is the ¼ mile long level siding to the hospital boiler house. The siding was sanctioned in 1887, extended in 1906 and closed in 1963 but the rails remained in position until 1988. (D. Cullum)

76. The standard CLASP building is seen in September 1973, soon after its completion, with the old lattice signal posts beyond. They disappeared soon after 'A' Box was closed on 8th September 1974. (J. Scrace)

77. The 10.00 Waterloo to Reading service arrives on 3rd August 1988, when the only item of antiquity was the footbridge. When the road bridge was rebuilt, it lost the panelling seen in earlier photographs. (J. Scrace)

LONGCROSS

78. Opened as a halt on 21st September 1942, it serves the nearby MOD depot, which is used for military vehicle testing. A siding to the depot passes under the gate seen at the end of the down platform on the right. It was in use from 8th November 1942 until 19th November 1961 and branched off from a trailing siding from the down line. (Lens of Sutton)

79. An up Ascot race special passes through on 21st June 1952, having passed Knowle West Box which was closed on 18th July 1971. One mile separated it from Knowle East Box, which ceased to function on 10th June 1969. Near its site, a siding was laid on the down side for the unloading of road aggregates for the M3 construction, from 1971 to 1974. (D. Cullum)

80. The hotel dominates this westward view from the main road, the station entrance being under the canopy on the left, neither displaying nameboards. The village was nearly a mile to the north but housing development has subsequently taken place nearer the station. (Lens of Sutton)

The 1914 survey shows the station's gasworks but not the position of the 4½ ton crane. The footbridge dated from 1890.

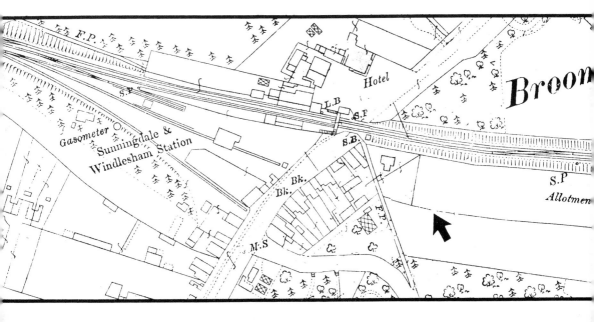

81. Looking west from the up platform we gain a glimpse of the goods shed. Situated between Chobham Common and Windsor Great Park, the pleasantly wooded area has been developed with many sizeable luxury dwellings, housing many potential 1st class ticket purchasers. (Lens of Sutton)

→ 83. The nearest building in this 1969 picture is the spacious gentlemen's toilet. The goods yard was on the right and, from 6th December 1965, it only handled coal traffic. It closed completely on 6th January 1969. (J. Scrace)

82. The suffix "& Bagshot" was added in 1863 and dropped in 1873, "& Windlesham" being used between 1893 and 1920. The signal box remained in use until 5th September 1975, having been reduced to function as a gate box twelve months earlier.
(Lens of Sutton)

84. The A30 trunk road is dual carriageway in the vicinity of the level crossing, which was equipped with half barriers in 1970. These were increased to four in 1975, prior to closure of the signal box and transfer of control to Feltham under CCTV. The photograph was taken in February 1971. (D. Cullum)

85. Following the provision of a CLASP building in 1973, the entrance was moved to the down side. The goods yard became a car park and was partially occupied by a supermarket, the roof of which is visible in the 1988 photograph. (J. Scrace)

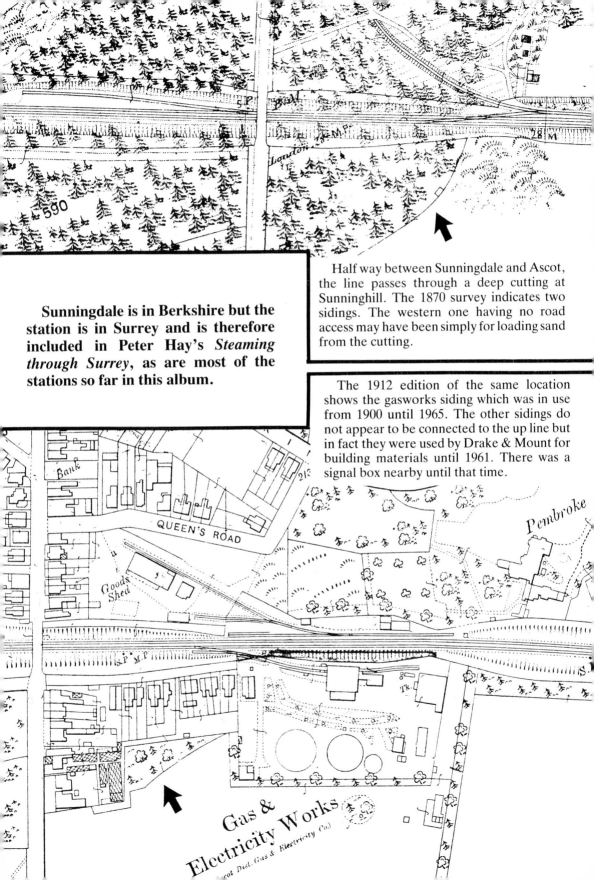

Half way between Sunningdale and Ascot, the line passes through a deep cutting at Sunninghill. The 1870 survey indicates two sidings. The western one having no road access may have been simply for loading sand from the cutting.

Sunningdale is in Berkshire but the station is in Surrey and is therefore included in Peter Hay's *Steaming through Surrey*, as are most of the stations so far in this album.

The 1912 edition of the same location shows the gasworks siding which was in use from 1900 until 1965. The other sidings do not appear to be connected to the up line but in fact they were used by Drake & Mount for building materials until 1961. There was a signal box nearby until that time.

4. Wokingham to Bracknell

WOKINGHAM

86. Wokingham had a station on the SER's Reading branch for seven years before the Ascot line was completed. This view north reveals the complex rodding outside the 1933 signal box. Before its commissioning, there had been one box at the junction and one near the goods yard. (Lens of Sutton)

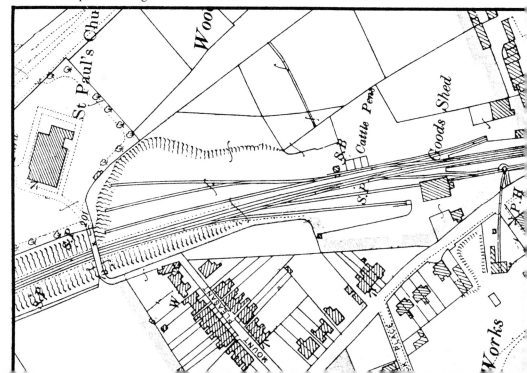

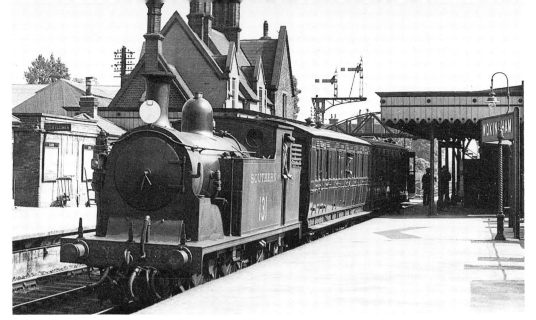

87. Class M7 0-4-4T no.131 waits with set no.733 and is seen standing at the down platform. The gothic style architecture was to be seen extensively on the former SER route to Redhill. (Lens of Sutton)

The 1899 edition includes three signal boxes, a short line running west into a brickworks and a narrow bridge (seen in picture 88) giving access exclusively to St. Pauls Church. The northern box was of SER origin, the middle box was for the crossing keeper and the one at the junction was worked by the LSWR.

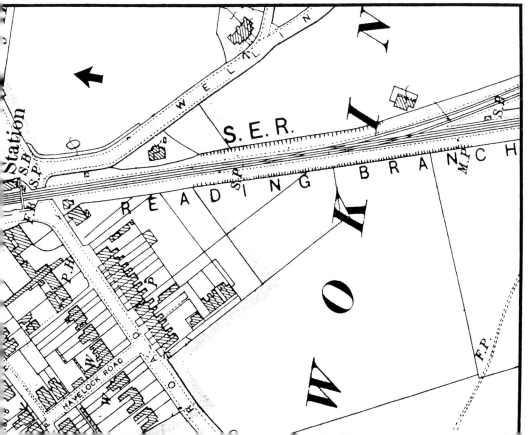

88. Class N 2-6-0 no. 31412 indicates that its train is a Reading to Margate service, on 1st August 1964. Part of the goods shed is visible on the left, there being three other freight sidings on each side of the main line at that time. (T. Wright)

89. Single line working was in force on 12th June 1966, following bridge bashing by a lorry at Earley. A 2BIL arrives "wrong road", while the following Waterloo service waits alongside to commence from Wokingham. Goods facilities were withdrawn on 6th January 1969, although the sidings were usable until 1972. (R.E. Ruffell)

90. Appearance was sacrificed for functional simplicity when a fresh building was brought into use in November 1973. A bridge was provided for passengers, the old double-head rail-built one being retained for public use. A 4CIG is seen departing for Waterloo via Ascot on 3rd July 1982. (A. Dasi-Sutton)

91. The 17.52 Theale to Northfleet train of empty cement tankers passes over Wokingham Junction on 7th September 1988, headed by no. 33056 *Burma Star* and no. 33051 *Shakespeare Cliff.* They catch the evening sun as the rear cars pass Wokingham Box, which then still controlled the junction points mechanically. The siding adjacent to the Guildford lines in the foreground was part of an emergency war time loop, formed in 1944 and usable as such until 1969. (J. Scrace)

For other maps and views of this station, see pictures 33 to 41 in our *Reading to Guildford* album.

0037
SOUTHERN RAILWAY.
Searchlight Tattoo.
Available as advertised.
Aldershot to
WOKINGHAM
First Class
FOR CONDITIONS SEE BACK
SOUTHERN RAILWAY.
Searchlight Tattoo.
Available as advertised.
Wokingham to
ALDERSHOT
First Class
0037

92. One mile east of the junction the Ascot line crosses the road to Crowthorne at Star Lane Crossing. It is seen on 18th June 1964, during the installation of automatic half barriers. The box had been a block post until August 1957. (D. Cullum)

93. Half a mile east of Star Lane is Waterloo Crossing, named after the nearby Waterloo Lodge. It was photographed in May 1965 and converted to automatic half barriers on 17th August 1965. (D. Cullum)

94. Officials inspect Amen Crossing on 13th May 1965, three months before it received AHBs. The crossing was closed permanently on 28th August 1982, following the re-routing of the A329 on a new bridge over the railway. (D. Cullum)

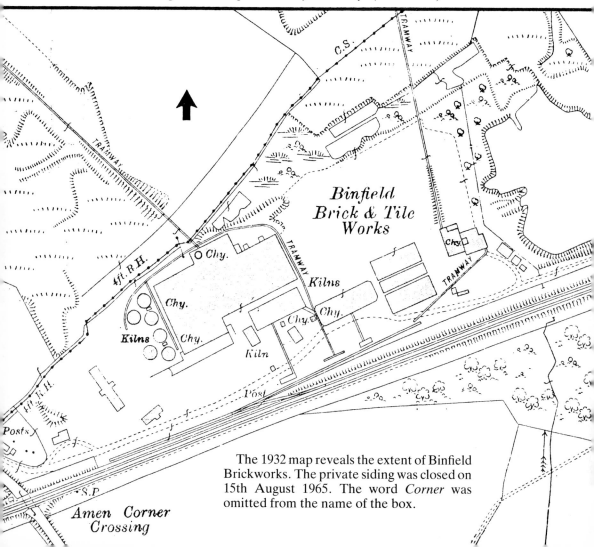

The 1932 map reveals the extent of Binfield Brickworks. The private siding was closed on 15th August 1965. The word *Corner* was omitted from the name of the box.

BRACKNELL

95. The small town was served by the only intermediate station between Wokingham and Ascot when the line opened. Two more road bridges and a footbridge have appeared over the cutting in recent years. (Lens of Sutton)

96. A slater is at work while the staff pose for a photograph of the north facade in deep shadow. Milk churn traffic originated from the extensive pasture land north of the town, which contrasts with the light sandy soils to the south. (Lens of Sutton)

97. Carriages wait in the station approach as horse boxes fill the sidings. The solitary box is in the short dock which had end and side loading facilities. The signal box remained in use until 27th January 1974. (Lens of Sutton)

The 1932 survey shows the goods yard and the down sidings at their optimum. Lower left is Manor Siding Box, which was a block post and was in use until 18th September 1955. Opposite it is the commencement of the siding to Down Mill Brick Works. Traffic ceased in January 1945, having started in 1899. Early in WWII, Bracknell accommodated an ambulance train, but in March 1941 it was moved to Horley. In 1949, the town of about 5000 inhabitants was designated an overspill area for London and, by 1989, the population had risen to over 52,000.

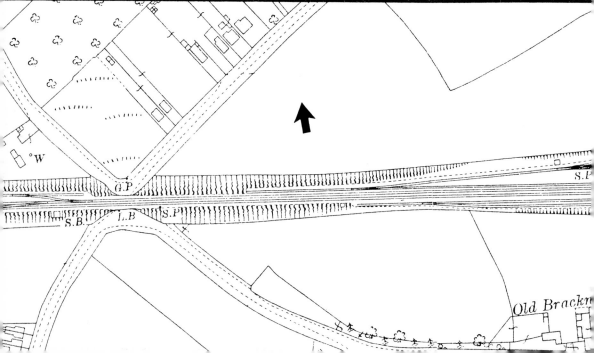

98. A temporary station and platform was erected on the up side in 1975, to allow construction of a new station on the site of the old one. Until 1970, there had been two down sidings, on the left. (R.E. Ruffell)

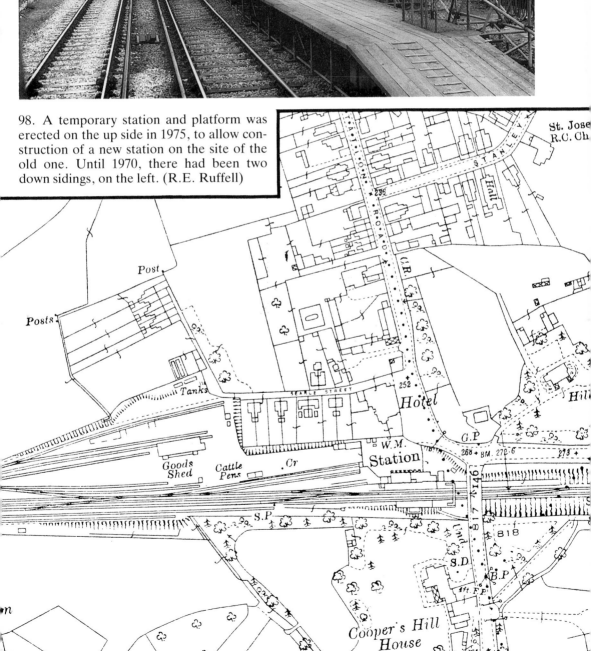

99. The new station included an extensive office block which, when photographed in 1988, was occupied by the car hire firm, Avis. A car park occupied the site of the goods yard, which was provided with a 7½ ton crane and closed on 6th January 1969. (J. Scrace)

100. A westward view in 1988 shows the replacement concrete footbridge, the down platform extension and one of the two down side shelters. Since May 1988, there has been a 20-minute interval service to Reading. (J. Scrace)

MARTINS HERON

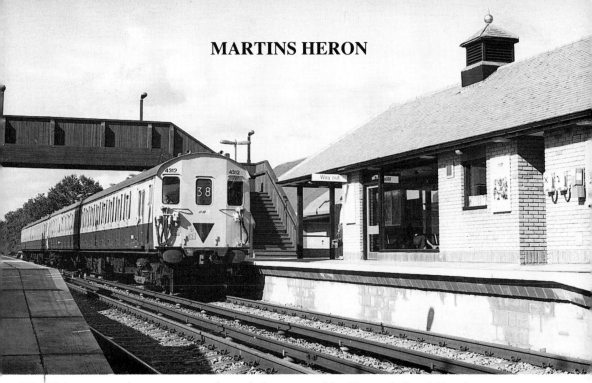

101. This new station was opened on 3rd October 1988, the cost of £500,000 having been jointly met by BR and Berkshire County Council. It was the eighth to be opened by Network SouthEast in two years and illustrated the great improvement in architecture since the boxes of the 1970s. (J. Scrace)

102. Another photograph taken a week after the opening shows the long roof of the adjacent supermarket. Extensive residential development has taken place since Martins Heron was an isolated country house, surrounded by the forest adjacent to Whitmoor Bog. Beyond the curve is a two mile straight to Ascot. (J. Scrace)

5. Ascot

ASCOT WEST

The two platforms and a bay were in use for race-traffic only until about 1968, passengers having to walk over a mile to the course. This 1912 map includes a private siding, on the left, which had served a brickworks since 1878. During WWI, an additional siding was laid to a Royal Flying Corps camp (RAF from January 1918). From 1931, Bertram Mills' Circus used two sidings adjacent to the down platform and a third line curved south to cross the A332. This reached Thomas Lawrence's Swinley Brickworks and was horse worked.

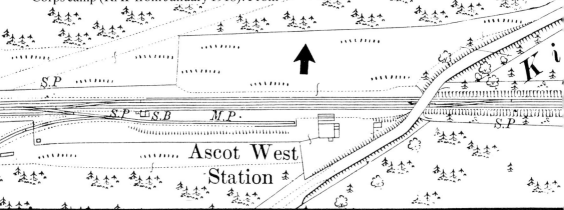

103. Each summer Bertram Mills hired vehicles from the various main line companies and then clipped on their own nameboards. In 1938, the LMS provided a number of horse boxes, this example having been built at Derby in 1935. Bogie luggage vans were hired for equipment and were fitted with bunks for some of the staff, as were some redundant LSWR corridor coaches. Flat bogie wagons (*MACAWS*) were used for wheeled cages for wild animals, while the elephants travelled in bogie vans with specially rated springs. (H.C. Casserley)

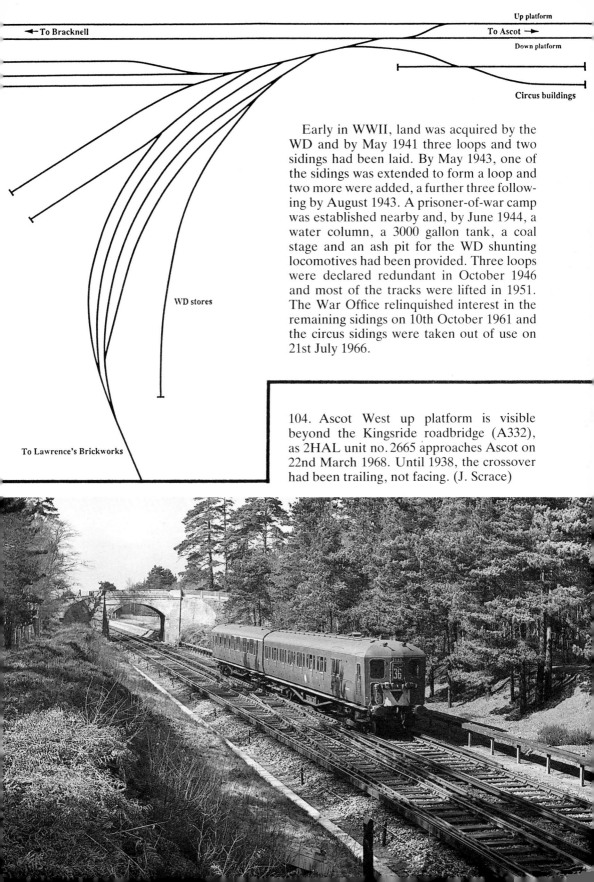

Up platform

◄— To Bracknell   To Ascot —►

Down platform

Circus buildings

WD stores

To Lawrence's Brickworks

Early in WWII, land was acquired by the WD and by May 1941 three loops and two sidings had been laid. By May 1943, one of the sidings was extended to form a loop and two more were added, a further three following by August 1943. A prisoner-of-war camp was established nearby and, by June 1944, a water column, a 3000 gallon tank, a coal stage and an ash pit for the WD shunting locomotives had been provided. Three loops were declared redundant in October 1946 and most of the tracks were lifted in 1951. The War Office relinquished interest in the remaining sidings on 10th October 1961 and the circus sidings were taken out of use on 21st July 1966.

104. Ascot West up platform is visible beyond the Kingsride roadbridge (A332), as 2HAL unit no. 2665 approaches Ascot on 22nd March 1968. Until 1938, the crossover had been trailing, not facing. (J. Scrace)

105. The signal box, seen in March 1968, was at the west end of the down platform and closed on 5th October 1969. In the background is part of the winter quarters for Bertram Mills Circus. (J. Scrace)

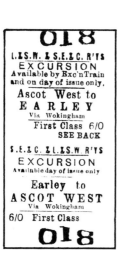

018

L.&S.W. & S.E.&C. R'ys
EXCURSION
Available by Exc'n Train
and on day of issue only.
Ascot West to
E A R L E Y
Via Wokingham
First Class 6/0
SEE BACK

S.E.&C. & L.&S.W. R'ys
EXCURSION
Available day of issue only
Earley to
ASCOT WEST
Via Wokingham
6/0 First Class

018

ASCOT RACE PLATFORM

106. To increase capacity, an additional up platform was provided between Ascot West and Ascot, which can be seen in the distance in May 1968. The platform ceased to be used at about this time. (J. Scrace)

ASCOT

107. The station was extended greatly when it became a junction in 1878, five platforms being provided with no. 1 having two faces. A subway still links them and connects directly with a ½ mile long footpath to the racecourse and not to the booking hall. Racing was started by Queen Anne in about 1711 and until WWII meetings were held for one week only each year. They have been more frequent subsequently. (Lens of Sutton)

The 1912 survey marks three signal boxes (S.B.) and two engine houses which housed pumps for the station water supply. The locomotive shed is outlined, lower left. The station was "Ascot and Sunninghill" from 1st February 1857 until 10th July 1921. The

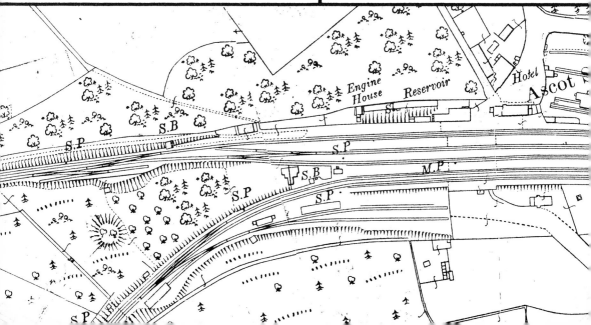

goods yard handled only coal after 11th July 1966 and closed completely on 6th January 1969, thereafter becoming a car park. By 1989, only an engineer's siding ran through platform 5 and no. 4 was trackless.

108. Looking east from platform 4 we witness the arrival of class F1 4-4-0 no. 1140, while class M7 0-4-4T takes water at platform 2, having propelled its coaches up the Bagshot line. The gantry crane behind it replaced a standard 5-ton model. This and the next three photographs were taken on 8th April 1938. (H.C. Casserley)

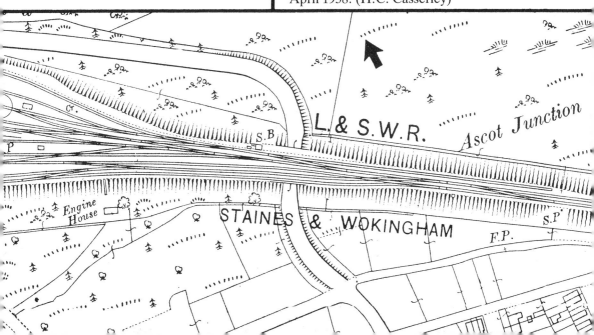

110. A look-out man is posted outside the Branch Box which was earlier known as South Box and which functioned only as a ground frame from 30th September 1928 until its closure on 16th October 1938. (H.C. Casserley)

109. On the left, a Farnham train stands at platform 5, the Branch Box being visible beyond it. On the right, circus vans stand at platform 2, which was then not used regularly by passenger trains. Until track rearrangements were completed in October 1938, Bagshot line trains could only use platforms 4 and 5. (H.C. Casserley)

111. Circus vans are shunted out of platform 2 by class 700 no. 699, the fourth one partially obscuring the water tank and the rear ones similarly treating West Junction Box, which closed on 9th September 1938.
(H.C. Casserley)

112. The RCTS duplicate Longmoor rail-tour is eased round the 12 chain curve into platform 4 by WD 2-10-0 Gordon on 30th April 1966. On the right is the former loco-motive coal stage. (R.E. Ruffell)

113. 2 BIL no. 2040 heads the 13.58 from Waterloo on 16th May 1969 and awaits division of the train. In the distance is 'A' Box, formerly East Junction Box, which remained in use until 24th July 1973. (J.H. Bird)

114. From 1938 until 1973, the northern part of the branch was quadruple track and con-nections were made to all platforms, nos. 1, 2 and 4 being signalled for reversible running. 'B' Box was opened on 16th October 1938, closed on 8th September 1974 and is seen at the end of platforms 3 and 4 on 19th May 1969, as the 2 BIL leaves for Reading, having shed its Guildford portion. (J.H. Bird)

115. The locomotive shed was erected in about 1890 and was only 70ft. long. Previously, a small shed had been provided close to the 50ft. turntable, which remained in the goods yard until around 1964. The shed was little used after 1936 and was demolished in 1969, shortly after this photograph was taken. (R.E. Ruffell)

116. The goods shed is visible above the second van, as an elephant is unloaded on 24th November 1968. By this time, circus activity was coming to an end and the Ascot West sidings were closed. For some while after arrival, elephants continued to sway, causing the vans to rock in the sidings. (R.E. Ruffell)

117. A look west in September 1971 shows the connection between platform 3 and the down main line which was removed two years later. Further minor changes took place in 1974, prior to the introduction of colour light signalling and reversible running through platforms 1, 2 and 3. (D. Cullum)

118. During Royal Ascot Week in 1974, a special from the London Midland Region arrived behind no. 47326, while another race train stands in platform 2. Racing continues to make a useful boost to railway income. (R.E. Ruffell)

BRITISH RAILWAYS (S)
PRIVILEGE RETURN
Valid One Month
Wokingham to
ROCHESTER
Via LWO
Third Class Fare 7/5
FOR CONDITIONS
SEE BACK
5073

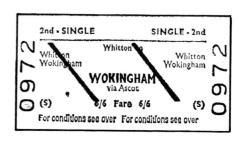

2nd · SINGLE   SINGLE · 2nd
0972   Whitton
Whitton   Whitton
Wokingham   Wokingham
WOKINGHAM
via Ascot
0972
(S)   6/6 Fare 6/6   (S)
For conditions see over For conditions see over

119. A serious fire in 1982 necessitated provision of a new roof over platform 1 and major renovation work to the building. This task was completed in August 1986. The 1877 exterior presented a good impression to impending passengers 111 years later. (J. Scrace)

120. The 13.32 departure stands at both faces of platform 1 on 5th August 1988, about to leave for Waterloo and calling at Richmond and Clapham Junction only. The lines around Ascot still offer the rail tourist some pleasant countryside and much evidence of a past railway era. (J. Scrace)

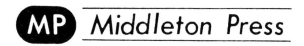

MP *Middleton Press*

Easebourne Lane, Midhurst, West Sussex, GU29 9AZ
☎ Midhurst (073 081) 3169

BRANCH LINES
BRANCH LINES TO MIDHURST
BRANCH LINES TO HORSHAM
BRANCH LINES TO ALTON
BRANCH LINE TO HAYLING
BRANCH LINE TO SOUTHWOLD
BRANCH LINE TO TENTERDEN
BRANCH LINES TO NEWPORT
BRANCH LINES TO TUNBRIDGE WELLS
BRANCH LINE TO SWANAGE
BRANCH LINES TO LONGMOOR
BRANCH LINES TO LYME REGIS
BRANCH LINES **AROUND** MIDHURST
BRANCH LINE TO FAIRFORD
BRANCH LINE TO ALLHALLOWS
BRANCH LINES AROUND ASCOT

SOUTH COAST RAILWAYS
CHICHESTER TO PORTSMOUTH
BRIGHTON TO EASTBOURNE
RYDE TO VENTNOR
EASTBOURNE TO HASTINGS
PORTSMOUTH TO SOUTHAMPTON
HASTINGS TO ASHFORD*
SOUTHAMPTON TO BOURNEMOUTH
ASHFORD TO DOVER
BOURNEMOUTH TO WEYMOUTH

COUNTRY RAILWAY ROUTES
BATH TO EVERCREECH JUNCTION
BOURNEMOUTH TO EVERCREECH JUNCTION
READING TO GUILDFORD
WOKING TO ALTON
GUILDFORD TO REDHILL

SOUTHERN MAIN LINES
WOKING TO PORTSMOUTH
HAYWARDS HEATH TO SEAFORD
EPSOM TO HORSHAM
CRAWLEY TO LITTLEHAMPTON
THREE BRIDGES TO BRIGHTON
WATERLOO TO WOKING
VICTORIA TO EAST CROYDON
TONBRIDGE TO HASTINGS
EAST CROYDON TO THREE BRIDGES
WOKING TO SOUTHAMPTON
WATERLOO TO WINDSOR
LONDON BRIDGE TO EAST CROYDON

STEAMING THROUGH
STEAMING THROUGH KENT
STEAMING THROUGH EAST HANTS
STEAMING THROUGH SURREY
STEAMING THROUGH WEST SUSSEX
STEAMING THROUGH THE
 ISLE OF WIGHT

OTHER RAILWAY BOOKS
WAR ON THE LINE
(Reprint of the SR history in World War II)
GARRAWAY FATHER AND SON
(Biography - includes LNER, Talyllyn and Festiniog Railways)
INDUSTRIAL RAILWAYS OF THE SOUTH-EAST

OTHER BOOKS
MIDHURST TOWN – THEN & NOW
EAST GRINSTEAD – THEN & NOW
THE MILITARY DEFENCE OF WEST SUSSEX
WEST SUSSEX WATERWAYS
SURREY WATERWAYS
BATTLE OVER PORTSMOUTH
A City at war in 1940
SUSSEX POLICE FORCES

*Video also available. Details from
M.P. Videos, 11 Park Crescent, Midhurst,
West Sussex GU29 9ED.